Original title:
The Spirit of Evergreen

Copyright © 2024 Creative Arts Management OÜ
All rights reserved.

Author: Elias Montgomery
ISBN HARDBACK: 978-9916-94-100-3
ISBN PAPERBACK: 978-9916-94-101-0

From Sapling to Sentinel

A tiny seedling, quite absurd,
It thought it was the funniest bird.
With roots that tickled, leaves like fans,
It danced around with giddy plans.

Tall friends would tease, they'd point and laugh,
But little one just found its path.
In time it grew, quite proud, to stand,
A mighty tree in nature's band.

Mysteries of the Hundred-Year Grove

In a grove so old, where legends hide,
Trees gossip secrets on the breeze side.
They play tic-tac-toe with their own twigs,
And giggle at humans who wear wigs.

One tree swears it's seen a ghost,
While others argue, "We saw it first!"
Branches sway to whisper tales,
Of silly squirrels in funny trails.

Alive in Eternal Embrace

Leaves whisper softly, a playful tease,
As wind tickles trunks, oh what a breeze!
They hug each other in nature's song,
Competing in twists to see who's strong.

Roots intertwine like best pals tight,
In a leafy dance, it's quite the sight.
With laughter echoing through the bark,
A comedy show from dawn till dark.

Footprints in a Green Oasis

Look at those prints, a curious sight,
Were they made by a cat or a sprite?
The trees chuckle, their leaves all sway,
While birds tweet jokes that brighten the day.

Nature's jesters play hide and seek,
With chipmunks stealing the shows each week.
In this oasis, all are quite merry,
As frogs in tuxedos sing to the cherry.

Whispers of Timeless Pines

In forests deep, the trees converse,
With squirrel gossip, oh, how they rehearse!
"Did you see that bird? It stole my seed!"
"Well, I once tripped over a playful weed!"

Their branches sway with laughter's tune,
As woodland critters dance 'neath the moon.
"I'm growing tall; you're quite the sprout!"
"Too bad your needles often fall out!"

Beneath Canopies of Green

The grass below is tickling toes,
As ants march by in their little rows.
"Excuse me, buddy, do I smell bad?"
"It's just the flowers, don't be sad!"

Lively leaves clap in a gentle breeze,
While chubby bunnies munch with ease.
"Did you hear about the snail's slow race?"
"Yeah, he took the wrong path, what a disgrace!"

The Evergreen Heartbeat

A pinecone dropped; it made a thud,
"Hey, watch it, buddy, don't be a dud!"
Said the moss to the rock, all shaded gray,
"You're just jealous 'cause I grow this way!"

The bark's got stories, wrapped in rings,
Of playful winds and the joy it brings.
"I'm not that old, just quite mature!"
"Yeah, right, you're just a funky dinosaur!"

Evergreen Echoes of Nature

In twilight whispers, shadows play,
While owls chuckle at the end of day.
"Who's that snoring in the tall oak tree?"
"Oh, just Grandpa Bear, he's always free!"

The foliage wiggles, having some fun,
As fireflies join in, one by one.
"Did you steal my light? You sneak!"
"Not me, pal, it was a little freak!"

Lush Memories of a Stalwart Grove

In the grove where squirrels chatter,
Acorns drop like rain of butter.
Trees wear hats of leafy green,
Their bark's the best you've ever seen.

Branches stretch like eager hands,
Dancing swiftly, making plans.
A wise old oak begins to snore,
While grasshoppers throw a dance-off encore.

Mossy cushions tickle beneath,
While tree frogs laugh till they bequeath.
With roots so deep, they tell a tale,
Of whispered jokes in a leafy gale.

So join the party, take a seat,
Join the trees for a tasty treat.
Nature's joke is evergreen fun,
Where laughter blossoms, second to none.

Infinitum of the Forest

In a wood where shadows play,
Trees gossip in their own ballet.
A raccoon wears a wizard's hat,
While owls debate, 'What's the best cat?'

The bushes grin with berry stains,
Dancers spin in twirling lanes.
Mushrooms laugh with colors bright,
In this wacky, wondrous sight.

A squirrel juggles pine cones high,
While birds claim they can touch the sky.
The breeze hums a jolly tune,
While bees buzz like a cartoon tune.

So stroll beneath these ancient towers,
Where laughter blooms like springtime flowers.
Every leaf has a funny quip,
In this realm, let joy be your grip.

Resilient Roots: A Silent Ode

Deep below where secrets lie,
Roots converse and sometimes sigh.
They share tales of thunderous storms,
And how they bend in playful forms.

Funky fungi join the scene,
With jokes that make the branches lean.
They giggle under the ground so wide,
While moles dig with a playful stride.

Wise old pines point to the stars,
Challenging beetles with their cars.
'Can you race us? Give it a try!'
Leaves rustle as laughter fills the sky.

Their silent ode a playful cheer,
In this woodland world, nothing to fear.
Let roots remind you every day,
Life's a giggle in its own way.

Embrace of the Verdant Soul

A tree in mid-shimmy, oh what a sight,
Shaking its branches with pure delight.
Leaves spin round like ballerinas,
Nature's dance, filled with sweet divinas.

Bushes whisper their cheeky tales,
Of daring deeds and funny fails.
In this grove where giggles flow,
Every branch has a tale to bestow.

Under the canopy's playful shade,
Laughter colors the daylight parade.
With roots entwined like best of friends,
In this wild world, the fun never ends.

So hop along, don't be shy,
Join the laughter, let spirits fly.
Cuz even in shadows, light finds its way,
Together we laugh, through night and day.

Labyrinths of Leafy Wonder

In the woods, I lost my way,
Chasing squirrels who wanted to play.
They circled 'round, a feathery court,
While I tripped over roots, oh what sport!

A bush with berries gave me a wink,
I tasted its fruit, and it made me blink.
Was that a goblin sipping on dew?
Or just a raccoon in a tutu?

Branches above began to groove,
Whispering secrets, they seemed to move.
A hedge maze spun my mind in knots,
And I wondered if grass had any thoughts.

As I laughed with the trees, they jested and spun,
Saying, "Join our take, this is all in fun!"
With mushrooms laughing and trees full of cheer,
I knew I'd return, time and time of year.

Nature's Inkwell of Resilience

A puddle reflected my wild-eyed grin,
While bees took bets on who'd dance and spin.
The daisies sighed, "Oh, what a day!"
As I trip-trapped about, in a most clumsy way.

Trees sat writing memoirs with bark,
Claiming their woes, lingering on the dark.
But what of the flowers? They laughed out loud,
"To bloom and to wilt, makes one so proud!"

The river tossed tales from its bubbling spree,
"Life is a joke! Come laugh with me!"
As birds chirped puns with a rhythmic flair,
I wondered if nature was writing a prayer.

With leaves as my pages, I'd pen my own tale,
Where humor and heart would surely prevail.
For in this ink well of laughter so bright,
I'd rise with the sun, and dance through the night.

Soaring Above, Roots Below

High above, the flutterers cheer,
Wings made of giggles fill the air near.
While down below in earthy embrace,
Worms tell tales of a subterranean race.

The wind took a spin, a wily old mate,
Said, "Why chase clouds when you can roller skate?"
As I looked to the sky, my sneakers unstrapped,
I turned on my heels, and whoomp! I had flapped!

The tree's bark chuckled, "You've got it all wrong,
Life's but a dance, so come join the throng!"
And the roots whispered secrets, corkscrewed and sly,
While I leapt and twirled as the branches waved high.

With laughter, we blended, both high and low,
Nature's own band played a merry-go-show.
So here's to the joy, found in every sprout,
Whether soaring with mirth, or cavorting about!

Kisses from the Canopy Above

Leaves whisper secrets to the breeze,
Swaying gently, teasing with ease.
A bird drops a twig, aiming for my hair,
I shake my fist in mock despair.

Branches giggle, holding up the sun,
Critters dance, oh what fun!
Squirrels recite poetry none can hear,
While I chuckle, sipping my root beer.

The trees are a comedy, watch them play,
Sprinkling laughter along the way.
Nature's jesters with green capes so bright,
Under their watch, every day feels right.

Legends of the Lush

In the boughs, tall tales are spun,
Of trees with mustaches and flowers that run.
A wise old oak claims he wore a crown,
But all we see is his bark wearing down.

Vines might argue, claiming to be kings,
Hanging around, boasting of their flings.
While daisies giggle and tell their own lore,
Stumbling over roots, they can't keep score.

Bees hum a tune to the beat of the night,
While frogs croak jokes, giving us a fright.
The legends of lush, all wild and absurd,
Leave us in stitches, each crazy word.

Breath of the Undying Green

Inhale the chuckles from the old pine trees,
Exhale giggles carried on the breeze.
Ferns share puns that tickle the floor,
While dandelions laugh, begging for more.

Moss gets cozy, telling stories at dusk,
Of frogs in tuxedos, all prim and brusque.
The laughter echoes in every green fold,
Making the forest feel younger, not old.

Roots intertwine like friends at a party,
While critters wear hats, looking quite hearty.
Breath of the green, such jesters abound,
In this parody palace, joy is profound.

A Tidal Wave of Foliage

A tidal wave hits, made of leafy delight,
Stocks of kale surfing, what a sight!
Lettuce lounges, soaking up rays,
While zany zucchini plays in the bays.

The flora convenes for a dance on the shore,
Petals pirouette, begging for more.
A cabbage shimmies, winking in glee,
And I can't help laughing at their jubilee.

The corn stalks sway with whimsical grace,
As veggies compete in this leafy race.
With each wave of laughter, the garden thrives,
In this bustling sea, nature truly jives.

The Essence of Endless Green

In a forest where jokes grow thick,
Trees wear hats, it's quite the trick.
Squirrels gossip in tiny knots,
While pinecones dance in silly spots.

Moss plays hide and seek all day,
While branches wave in a quirky way.
Leaves laugh as they flutter down,
Creating a soft, green-kissed crown.

Bark gives puns that make us cheer,
As roots tap dance, loud and clear.
Nature's humor, a playful spree,
In a world where laughter's free.

So come along, bring a grin,
In this green realm, let the fun begin!
Amidst the laughter, joy takes flight,
Endless green, a pure delight.

Guardians of the Whispering Woods

In the woods where giggles grow,
Dancing trees steal the show.
Acorns chuckle as they drop,
While rabbits hop and never stop.

Owls wear glasses, wise yet wild,
With every hoot, they act like a child.
Deer make faces, oh what a scene,
In these woods painted in green.

Mushrooms sporting little hats,
Join a band of singing bats.
All the critters twirl around,
In this kingdom where fun is found.

So take a bow, to nature's jest,
In every tree, a stand-up fest.
Guardians of laughter, bushes that sway,
In this jolly place, let's play all day.

A Lullaby of Evergreen Shadows

In the twilight, shadows play,
Boughs croon songs in a funny way.
The moon chuckles at the scene,
As branches sway, leafy and green.

Night critters join in the tune,
With fireflies buzzing like a cartoon.
Raccoons laugh, their smiles wide,
In this cozy, shady slide.

Whispers of trees tickle the night,
While cicadas hum, a silly flight.
Each rustle brings a giggle bright,
In shadows where laughter takes flight.

So drift away on a giggling breeze,
Beneath the stars, the rustling leaves.
With laughter guarding every dream,
In these shadows, joy's the theme.

The Resilience of Nature's Veil

In a world that giggles and grins,
Nature's cloak has many wins.
Soft ferns prance as if to tease,
While flowers whisper jokes with ease.

Breezes carry chuckles near,
Every rustle, a whispered cheer.
Cacti wear smiles, sharp but sweet,
While daisies dance on happy feet.

Through storms and laughter, they persist,
Nature's humor is hard to resist.
Let's celebrate with each silly fray,
A leafy party, come what may.

So raise a toast to green so bold,
With jokes and giggles; let's break the mold.
In this resilient, fun-filled gale,
Nature's laugh is our holy grail.

Chronicles of the Conifers

In the forest, trees do prance,
With roots that jiggle, they love to dance.
Squirrels chase and chipmunks cheer,
While the owls chuckle, "Oh dear, oh dear!"

Pine cones rain down, a crunchy shower,
Each branch a stage, each leaf a flower.
The trunks all gossip, stand tall and proud,
Making jokes that would brighten a crowd.

They whisper secrets in the breeze,
As raccoons giggle among the leaves.
Life's a comedy up in these trees,
Where even the branches tease with ease!

So let us laugh beneath their shade,
Where every creature's a part of the parade.
With nature's humor, we all unwind,
In the forest's quirks, true joy we find.

Lush Canopies and Silent Blessings

Under the greens, the laughter grows,
Where every twig has tales to disclose.
The vines twist and curl like a grand parade,
While the wind joins in, a playful charade.

Nature's playground, oh what a sight,
Where birds throw parties, day and night.
Each leaf a dancer, swaying with glee,
Chasing the bugs like it's a spree!

Mossy cushions like a giant bed,
Frogs sing lullabies, the sky overhead.
A squirrel's acrobatics can't be outdone,
In this crazy circus, we're all having fun!

So join the revelry, come take a peek,
In the woods' laughter, we find the peak.
With each rustle and giggle, let's not be shy,
In nature's embrace, happiness is nigh.

Guardians of the Woodlands

Timber tall with quirky flair,
Barking jokes, they fill the air.
Saplings giggle with each gust,
While wise old oaks say, "In trunks we trust!"

The moss is soft, like nature's grin,
While critters play at the branches' kin.
Rabbits hop, raccoons parade,
In this wild kingdom, friendships are made.

Cone-bearing jesters, all in a line,
Sharing their humor with a pinch of pine.
Every rustle sings a rhyme,
Crafting memories that bloom with time.

So here's to trees, guardians grand,
With laughter sprouting from every strand.
In their leafy embrace, we take our stance,
Joining the revelry, let's dance, let's dance!

Across the Seasons of Solace

In spring, the branches stretch and yawn,
Every leaf a jester, teasing the dawn.
They tickle the skies with new green glee,
As flowers burst forth for a jubilee!

Summer's sun brings a leafy laugh,
With shade as cool as a watermelon bath.
The bees are buzzing, a merry crew,
While the trees sway along, with a shimmy or two.

Autumn's colors are a comic show,
As leaves tumble down, a vibrant glow.
Every gust of wind, a playful fling,
The woods become a painted spring!

Winter wraps it in fluffy white,
As branches wear crowns, a dazzling sight.
Snowmen dance with hats made of bark,
In the forest's theater, igniting the spark!

Memories of the Unfading Grove

In a grove where trees dance and sway,
A squirrel once thought it could play.
He donned a mask, oh what a sight,
But fell from a branch, oh what a fright!

A wise old owl, with spectacles on,
Said, "Fake it till you make it, my fawn!"
Yet every night, that fella snores,
While critters host grand disco tours.

The acorns dropped, a wacky drum,
The leaves play tunes that make us hum.
A raccoon juggles, a showman's flair,
While chipmunks giggle without a care.

In this woodland, laughter fills the air,
With every stumble, every dare.
The memories linger in sunlit glows,
In this old grove, where fun always flows.

Glimmers of Life in Shade's Hold

Under shading leaves that twist and twine,
A grasshopper sings, claiming it's fine.
But who would think he'd miss his cue,
As butterflies laughed, 'We're not like you!'

The fireflies glow like little stars,
While beetles cruise in fancy cars.
A ladybug lost her sense of style,
She wore stripes, but thought it was a smile.

A snail in a race, oh what a feat,
Said, "Slow and steady can't be beat!"
But everyone else passed him by,
With speed so fast, he sighed with a sigh.

Together they laugh under moonlit skies,
In this shade, there are no goodbyes.
Each glimmering moment, a treasure to hold,
Where even the dull shine bright, oh so bold!

Enchanted Canopy of Ages

Beneath an arc of branches wide,
A raccoon's dance with no sense of pride.
He tripped on roots, oh what a fall,
While echoes of laughter filled the hall.

The trees whispered secrets of days long gone,
Of creatures who danced 'til the break of dawn.
And each leaf giggled, a jolly crew,
As they painted the air in every hue.

A wise old toad in a dapper hat,
Said, "Life is funny, just look at that!"
With a chuckle and croak, he led the way,
In this enchanted realm where fun holds sway.

Time ticks slowly, or not at all,
For laughter can make the mundane enthrall.
In every shade, a story unfolds,
As the canopy keeps its secrets bold.

Petals of Perseverance

In a garden where daisies twist and spin,
A sunflower grins, letting the fun begin.
He swayed with pride, tall as can be,
While buzzing bees tapped their dance decree.

A potted plant challenged every doubt,
With roots so strong, it shouted, "Check me out!"
But a gust of wind sent it to a whirl,
With petals tossed like a dizzy girl.

The veggie patch threw a grand buffet,
Where carrots and peas had a lively play.
A radish slipped, oh what a splatter,
While herbs rejoiced, "Does it even matter?"

Each bloom chuckled, through obstacles faced,
In this garden of laughter, joy is embraced.
With petals that shine in the brightest hues,
This place of resilience offers endless views.

An Ode to Immortal Green

In a forest where no one sweeps,
The moss grows thick, and silence creeps.
Yet squirrels jest, with acorn hats,
And dance around like clever brats.

In shades of jade, they spin and twirl,
While roots are tangled in a whirl.
The trees chuckle at the scene,
For nothing thrives like this bright green.

A snail in slow motion, it zips,
While birds drop snacks from lofty tips.
Nature's joke, oh what a treat,
With laughter echoing, quite sweet!

So here's to leaves that never fall,
They stand so tall, they mock us all.
With every tick of time's own clock,
These greens will play their timeless rock.

Chronicles Among the Cedars

Among the cedars, tall and proud,
A wise old owl hoots rather loud.
With every story, he takes a stand,
A comedy act in leafy land.

Raccoons in masks plan their heists,
Stealing snacks like bandit knights.
While chipmunks race in a quirky spree,
Chasing echoes, full of glee.

A gust of wind brings tales anew,
Of pinecone pirates and foggy dew.
Giggles rustle through branches high,
As nature's laughter fills the sky.

So heed the stories that trees have spun,
Where every creature has its fun.
In this green world, they hold the key,
To endless jest and harmony.

Tides of Time in Ferns' Flow

Ferns wave gently in breezy cheer,
As crickets chirp for all to hear.
Their leafy fingers tickle ground,
In this green mess, joy can be found.

A hedgehog rolls in endless play,
While butterflies tease on sunny day.
They flutter and zigzag in delight,
A nature dance that's pure and bright.

Each moment's wacky, none's the same,
In this green realm, it's all a game.
With laughter echoing, oh what fun,
Time's a friend, it never runs.

So let the ferns tell tales so fine,
Of joyous pranks in line and vine.
In every green nook, laughter flows,
The more you look, the more it grows.

The Peaceful Poise of Pines

The pines wear crowns, pointy and neat,
While squirrels scamper with quickening feet.
A chipmunk peeks from a snug little hole,
In this serene, yet funny role.

With branches swaying, they seem to sway,
As if they mock the sunny day.
Their boughs are heavy with whispered dreams,
And jokes afloat in their leafy streams.

A woodpecker taps with rhythm divine,
While pine nuts are tossed like birthday wine.
The forest groans with laughter's delight,
In every rustle, it's pure sight.

So cherish these giants thick and wise,
With silly antics in green disguise.
For in this woodland, where laughter rains,
You'll find true joy that forever remains.

Echoing Footsteps on Green Ground

In the woods where squirrels dance,
A rabbit hops with a silly prance.
They laugh and tease, a funny game,
While my shoes squeak—they're to blame!

Mice hold meetings in the trees,
Discussing cheese with such great ease.
Their tiny suits and hats askew,
They toast to life with nuts, it's true!

The bushes chuckle, branches sway,
A woodpecker starts his own cabaret.
Twirling leaves like confetti toss,
In this lush tale, I'm the boss!

So let's all frolic, jump, and shout,
For nature's laughter, without a doubt.
With each step on this grassy ground,
Echoes of joy and giggles abound!

Veins of Earth and Sky

Up above, the clouds wear hats,
While roots below host dancing rats.
They waltz beneath the sunny light,
In suits of dirt, what a sight!

The sunbeam tickles every leaf,
A giggling breeze, beyond belief.
The flowers blush, they start to sway,
In fashion shows, they steal the day!

Worms tell jokes, and they crack up,
While ladybugs sip from their cup.
A butterfly joins in the fun,
Dancing 'round like it's a run!

So look around, take in this spree,
Nature laughs, so wild and free.
In this realm of giggles galore,
Veins of joy forever soar!

Harmony in Each Needle's Touch

Pinecones drop with a thud, a blast,
While needles tickle as they pass.
A squirrel spins, caught in the rush,
He flips and tumbles—oh, what a hush!

The branches sway, they can't contain,
A chorus sings, but it's quite insane.
With rustling leaves and candor bright,
Every step feels just so light!

Ants march on, with tiny bags,
Collecting snacks for future stags.
They giggle as they proudly boast,
"I bring the cheese! You bring the toast!"

So dance along, feel every scratch,
In this green patch, there's quite the match.
With laughter woven in the trees,
Nature jokes—oh, what a tease!

Enigma of the Endless Foliage

Among the leaves, a riddle's spun,
Where jokers gather just for fun.
The branches gossip, telling tales,
Of hidden treasures and playful snails.

The vines entwine in a silly twist,
As buzzing bees join the humorous list.
With each flap, they spin and whirl,
They mix up words—oh, how they twirl!

An owl hoots, "What's the punchline here?"
The trees all chuckle as they lean near.
With shadows dancing, let's rejoice,
For every rustle lends a voice!

So wander through this quest so grand,
Where laughter sprinkles like fine sand.
In the mystery, let humor thrive,
In this green wonder, we come alive!

Sagas of Evergreen Solitude

In a forest deep, where pinecones roam,
A squirrel once claimed a wooden home.
He invited friends, like a dazzling show,
Yet forgot to mention the big fat crow.

Jokes flew like leaves, oh what a sight,
As trees swayed gently, in their delight.
A frog croaked loud, a stand-up chat,
But all the punchlines were lost to the cat.

They debated long on acorn wealth,
While pretending to boast about their health.
The beavers laughed, tails slapping away,
As the elder tree sighed, just another day.

A Canvas of Leafy Serenity

With leaves all around, so vibrant, so bright,
An artist with paint splatters took flight.
He slipped on a branch, made a colorful mess,
Leaving the forest in quite a distress.

The blossoms giggled, twirling about,
While the bushes whispered, "What's that about?"
When his canvas got wet, he squeaked in a sigh,
The wildflowers bloomed, "You should just fly!"

A chipmunk strutted, with nuts on his head,
Grinning like mad, he sat on a bed.
Creating a scene of comedic delight,
Nature's own joke, both silly and bright.

Whispers Among the Evergreen Fronds

Beneath the canopy, secrets unfold,
Where ferns gossip bright, with stories retold.
A bashful old owl hooted with cheer,
"Who did what?" the bushes would jeer.

The brook splashed along with a giggling trick,
As the rocks rolled their eyes at the elf with the stick.
Springtails danced with mischievous glee,
While ants plotted pranks, oh how they agree!

A twig snapped loud as laughter roared,
The maple sighed with humor stored.
The sun peeked in, with a wink from above,
As all of them dreamed of a life full of love.

The Language of the Leafy Elders

The ancient trees spoke in gnarled tongue,
Of near-miss acorns and when laughter sprung.
Their branches swayed to the wind's good jest,
While birds sat listening, feeling quite blessed.

Lichen and moss chimed in with a grin,
In jokes so old, where could one begin?
The nutty walnuts were cracking smart,
Arguing why they played the best part.

In a world that spun with leaves all around,
The echoes of laughter were joyfully found.
Though wisdom was shared through a chuckle or two,
In the forest's heart, there's always room for you.

Echoes Through the Canopy

In a forest where squirrels jeer,
Tall trees whisper secrets near.
They giggle at raccoons' attempts to sing,
While frogs dance in their own weird fling.

The owls hoot jokes at the stars so bright,
As fireflies twinkle, giving a fright.
Leaves rustle laughter as breezes blow,
In this silly abode where wonders grow.

Bark-wearing creatures form a parade,
Swinging their limbs in a leafy charade.
Who knew trees were such comedians?
With roots so deep, they're full of opinions!

So trek through the woods with a grin on your face,
Join in the humor of this thriving place.
For nature's a jest, a playful old sage,
And every green leaf is the best of a page.

Ageless Leaves in Twilight

As dusk drapes the woods in a cozy shawl,
Leaves chuckle softly, having the best ball.
They tickle the winds with their vibrant glee,
And tease the branches, 'Come dance with me!'

A wise old oak shares tales of his youth,
Of chipmunk pranks and the path to truth.
While ferns throw a party, not one leaf shy,
Inviting all critters, 'Come give it a try!'

Moss slips and slides just like a slick fool,
Hiding beneath roots, breaking all the rules.
And just as the sky begins to grow dim,
A chorus of crickets starts singing a whim.

Twilight giggles, the stars join in too,
With the moon peeking down, giving a view.
In the woodland of jokes where no heart can be grieved,
Forever they jest, forever believed.

Songs of Ancient Pines

Pine needles rustle underfoot's tread,
Making music like the best band ever bred.
And cones drop like cymbals with a clatter,
'This gig's so good, who cares about chatter?'

Nearby, a raccoon rehearses his show,
Wearing pinecones like hats, stealing the glow.
The saplings are rolling in laughter and cheer,
While squirrels critique, 'That act's less than clear!'

Above, the branches sway to the beat,
As the winds blow by, they dance on their feet.
A woodpecker plays the drum on a trunk,
Declaring, 'This jam's got the best little funk!'

Echoing laughter fills every nook,
This tree-top symphony, come have a look.
Nature's a jokester, with humor so fine,
In the songs of pines, we find ourselves twined.

Heartbeat of the Forest

In the depths of the woods, where shadows play,
Trees bounce to a rhythm that's here to stay.
A heartbeat of laughter, so loud and so clear,
Leaves wave as they giggle, 'Come join us, dear!'

Beneath every branch, a tale unfolds,
Of crickets who prank and owls who scold.
The cedar's old voice croons wisecracks so slick,
While bees buzz the chorus -- it's all quite a trick!

The mushrooms all gather for tea and some fun,
Comparing their sizes, 'I'm bigger, you pun!'
And just when you think it's quiet up here,
A rabbit pipes up, claiming, 'I'm the best deer!'

In this merry realm where the wildlings frolic,
The heart of the forest beats humor so melodic.
Each rustle and giggle, a reminder so true,
That joy's in the woods, in all that we do.

The Resilient Heart of Green

In a garden where laughter grows,
Plants gossip beneath the sun's warm shows.
Silly daisies dance in their patch,
Rolling leaves wave, then they scratch.

Whispers of roots tickle the earth,
Sunflowers giggle, it's all they're worth.
A squirrel steals acorns, thinks he's a king,
Wearing a crown made of leafy bling.

Laughter sprouts from flowers so bright,
Tulips twirl in the soft, warm light.
Beneath a bloom, a gnome takes a nap,
Dreaming of pies and a berry-filled lap.

Breezes chuckle as branches sway,
Nature's humor in full display.
So come, let's join in this leafy cheer,
Where every plant knows joy and beer!

Reflections Beneath the Tall Trunks

Underneath the trees so tall,
Shadows play, giggling, they sprawl.
A squirrel drinks from a funky cup,
While acorns tumble and roll up.

Moss has a party on bark so grand,
With tree frogs clapping, oh, isn't it planned?
Roots tell tales that make you roar,
As bugs parade on the forest floor.

Sunlight twinkles like a wink,
Leaves mimic giggles, pause, and think.
A wise old owl says, 'What a fun mess!'
As he wears a hat made of fern, no less!

In this place where laughter peeks,
Whispers and jests weave through the creeks.
So come take a seat, join the fun,
Under the trees, where all's never done!

Stories Woven in Ferns

Ferns spin tales of frolic and play,
Of wormy winks and dirt-throwing fray.
They shimmy and shake, no shame in sight,
In a tangle of giggles, a wild delight.

Once a beetle wore a tiny hat,
Complimented by a jolly old rat.
"Fancy that!" said the ladybug loud,
As she called them up to join the crowd.

Underneath curls where dew droplets tease,
Frogs in tuxedos groove to the breeze.
Grasshoppers burst into silly ballet,
Put on a show for the bugs every day.

The ferns all nod as rain starts to fall,
Each droplet a laugh, oh, they'll have a ball.
They'll dance with the wind until the sun dips,
With stories alive in their leafy scripts!

Dreams Drenched in Dew

Morning mist with a sparkle and gleam,
Plants stretch out, lost in a dream.
A snail races slow, taking its time,
While daisies play hopscotch, oh, so sublime.

Raindrops shake on leaves like a joke,
Mushrooms giggle, let's get a cloak!
In a world of whimsy where nothing's a bother,
Every bud hums to its leafy mother.

A toad croaks wisdom, wearing a tie,
While caterpillars share gossip nearby.
With butterflies fluttering in high-flying cheer,
Every moment feels just like a beer.

So float with the dew, let your cares go,
Join the frolic with all that you know.
For in this jolly realm, joy is anew,
With laughter and light, beneath the fresh dew!

Unity with the Understory

In the shadows where critters play,
Fungi giggle, come join the fray!
Mossy mats and whispers sweet,
Dancing roots beneath our feet.

Squirrels gossip, find a stash,
While ants march by with a bash.
A squirrel's acorn, a toad's delight,
Their quirky tales keep night so bright.

Every leaf has a job to do,
While busy beetles scuttle through.
In this green world, let's share a grin,
Finding joy in what lies within.

So take a peek, and don't be shy,
Under your feet, the fun piles high!
Living life right down below,
Where laughter stirs the soil's glow.

A Lament for Fallen Leaves

Oh leaf, you danced; now you're flat,
Once a crown, now just a mat.
Wind's great jokes cut you to ribs,
With every gust, a dusty fib.

Golden glories slipping down,
Crispy confetti upon the ground.
Was that a crunch, or just a sigh?
Whispers of trees, a cheeky guy.

"Regrets, regrets!" an oak does moan,
"Why'd you roll away from your throne?"
Yet here they gather, a colorful parade,
For every drop, a brand-new charade.

So laugh with me, don't shed a tear,
In this cascade, there's nothing to fear!
Leaves may fall, but fun's in the air,
A leafy jest—who really cares?

Majestic Roots, Reaching Deep

Roots tickle one another's toes,
Under ground, the laughter flows.
Whispers echo, "Look at me!"
"I've found a worm, it's quite a spree!"

Tangled tales and squiggly threads,
Join the club, where no one dreads.
Fungi's laughter, worm's delight,
They hold a party every night.

Each branch above sends down a cheer,
"Faster, faster, come gather near!"
Nature's wiggle is a grand ballet,
As giddy roots find a new way to play.

Throw down your worries, don't be shy,
Join the roots, we'll dance nearby!
So let's connect from stem to knee,
In our underground jubilee!

Stillness Amongst the Trees

In tranquil woods where silence hums,
The trees pull pranks, and laughter drums.
One sways left while the other leans,
Gossiping softly behind the scenes.

A woodpecker bursts into chuckles,
As squirrels plot their nutty buckles.
Crickets chirp their rhythmic sound,
Underneath, the laughter's found.

But hold on tight, it's now a race!
The wind joins in, a cheeky chase.
Branches swish with whispers bold,
In quiet moments, mirth unfolds.

So sit quite still, soak in the spree,
Among the leaves, feel wild and free!
Nature's jesters, up in the trees,
Keeping us smiling on the breeze.

Threads of Time in Green

In the grass, a squirrel danced,
His acorns stashed, all well-planned.
He tripped upon a wayward leaf,
Now he's stuck—oh, what a thief!

The trees giggled, rustling leaves,
As he schemes, like a man who weaves.
A tapestry of nature's jest,
The fashion's weird, but he thinks it's best.

The vines would tease, 'Come try a swing!'
Yet on that rope, his pants took wing.
He landed with a flourish, hooray!
This is just another funny day.

So if you see him prancing near,
With twigs and twine, and some green gear,
Remember all the laughs we share,
In threads of time with nature's flair.

Secret Dialogues with Moss

Underfoot, the moss has dreams,
It whispers softly, or so it seems.
'Hey there, ground, do you even care?
My fuzzy back needs some fresh air!'

The rocks just chuckle, 'Oh, what a plight,
To think you're cool after a rain-soaked night!'
The moss replies, 'Oh, I'm quite chic,
In this damp world, I'm unique!'

Here comes a snail with a puzzled look,
He hears their chat while munching a hook.
'In this grand scheme of trees and streams,
Am I the fool with my slimy dreams?'

But moss just smiles, 'Oh, don't you fret,
With style and slime, you ain't seen yet.'
They bonded over nature's joke,
As rains rolled in, the laughter woke.

Timeless Shade of the Pines

Beneath the pines, a shadow fights,
With squirrels clad in leafy tights.
They argue over acorns' worth,
One claims it's solid gold from Earth!

A crow flew by and yelled with glee,
'You mighty pines, can't you just see?
It's all a scheme you've missed from birth,
That acorn's worth is really just mirth!'

The pines chuckled, swaying slow,
'These little fights put on a show.
Let nature's humor fill the air,
In timeless shade, we've not a care!'

So if you stroll beneath those trees,
And hear them laugh in the gentle breeze,
Know that wisdom wears a grin,
While nature's quirks usher fun within.

Hushed Whispers of the Woods

In the woods where whispers twirl,
A raccoon plots, giving a whirl.
'Let's raid the picnic, oh what a treat!
With sticky paws and nothing to eat!'

The owls roll eyes at such a mess,
'Be more clever, or you'll confess!
Stealing crumbs is low in rank,
These humans leave us food, give thanks!'

The bushes rustle, an echo gleeful,
As birds join in, their tone deceitful.
'Oh raccoon dear, so pdized and spry,
Why not ask them to share some pie?'

Thus, nature plays its quirky game,
As laughter echoes, none to blame.
In hushed whispers where secrets lay,
The woods remind us to play each day.

Evergreen Reverie

In the forest, trees do dance,
With squirrels practicing their prance.
Each branch a stage, each leaf a song,
Nature's music, where we all belong.

A pinecone falls, what a silly sound,
As birds make jokes, all around.
The rabbits hop in a comical race,
With a tortoise rolling, keeping pace.

The sun winks down, a golden leer,
While mushrooms giggle, spreading cheer.
Sappy tales in the woodwind's play,
Sparkling laughter brightens the day.

So let us twirl in this leafy glee,
For life is full of leafy spree.
A chuckle from nature, wild and free,
In our hearts, we always agree.

Eternal Embrace of Nature

Bees buzz like they own the day,
As daisies wink, 'Come out and play!'
A rambling brook sings a silly tune,
While frogs leap high, over the moon.

The sun shines bright, like a goofy grin,
Crickets chirping, let the fun begin!
With vines that twine, in such a mess,
Nature laughs, she loves to impress.

A wind blows by, tickles the trees,
"Dance with me!" whispers the breeze.
With leaves that shimmy, a leafy jig,
"Come on folks, let's all dance big!"

In this world where smiles abound,
Laughter echoes all around.
Join the chaos, the joy we seek,
In nature's arms, we play hide and peek.

The Veil of Verdant Dreams

In a leafy realm where giggles sprout,
The flowers gossip, there's never a drought.
A playful breeze spins stories untold,
While ants march in lines, oh so bold.

Butterflies wear their brightest suits,
Tickling the petals, oh what a hoot!
A ladybug laughs, "Oh me, oh my,
Just trying to make my spots fly by!"

Trees tell tales of joys and woes,
Each knot and gnarled branch, a funny pose.
While fish in streams do backflips galore,
Nature's circus, who could ask for more?

In this carnival of the greenest hue,
Laughter echoes in every view.
Let's join the fun, and frolic too,
In this world where joy is due.

A Tapestry of Everlasting Life

In the garden where goofballs grow,
The puns and poodles steal the show.
Pumpkins laugh in the autumn sun,
Whispering secrets about the fun.

With grass that tickles your wandering feet,
Dancing daisies find the beat.
Bumblebees bumble with style and grace,
Trying their best not to fall on their face.

Clouds roll in, a fluffy parade,
Sprinkling raindrops, like a jester's charade.
The flowers gulp, "Here comes the fun!"
As puddles form, our laughter's begun.

So raise a cheer for the silly and bright,
In this tapestry where joy takes flight.
With every stitch, a giggle or two,
In nature's embrace, laughter's anew.

The Canvas of an Unfading World

In a meadow of colors, we laugh and we play,
The daisies wear sunglasses, it's a bright sunny day.
The wind whispers secrets, the trees roll their eyes,
As squirrels dress in feathers, a surprising disguise.

With colors that pop, like a tie-dye surprise,
The flowers all giggle as bees buzz nearby.
While the rabbits hold hands, doing a funky jig,
The butterflies flutter, twirling in a big swig.

The clouds play peek-a-boo, hiding with glee,
As ants form a conga line, oh look at them flee!
This canvas of laughter, where nature's a clown,
Paints the world with joy, never wears a frown.

Messages Carved in Bark

On an oak's rough surface, a message appears,
'Beware of the raccoon who drinks too many beers!'
Squirrels take bets on who'll win the next race,
While birds tweet their gossip, snickering with grace.

A pine has a note: 'I'm the tallest, hooray!'
And the lilacs all chuckle at the bad jokes they say.
They write of their dreams, with twigs as their pens,
In a world full of laughter, where humor never ends.

There's even a cedar, a prankster at heart,
Hiding acorns from squirrels, playing a funny part.
They chuckle in whispers, in this noble old park,
Where laughter is carved deep in the bark.

Serenades Among the Green Giants

Amidst leafy giants, a chorus arises,
With frogs croaking tunes that rival the prizes.
The crickets play drums, while the fireflies dance,
Creating a concert, it's nature's romance.

The elves strum guitars made of twigs and of leaves,
As raccoons in tuxedos play the bells with ease.
The owls hoot the melody, wise and quite bold,
While the breeze tickles everyone, as the night unfolds.

Unexpectedly, a badger joins in,
His tambourine shaking, causing giggles and grins.
The laughter resounds through the cool, fragrant night,
As the green giants sway, reveling in delight.

A Journey through the Timeless Grove

Let's wander together where the tall shadows play,
With mushrooms on stilts putting on their ballet.
The leaves tell old tales in a rustly tone,
While the giggling brook chuckles, never alone.

Each tree is a storyteller, with branches outspread,
Reciting old fables where legends have tread.
The path is a charmer, with stories so spry,
Filled with whimsy and laughter, as time flutters by.

A bridge made of pebbles, a snail starts to race,
While a porcupine grins, a slow-moving ace.
In this timeless grove, where every step's light,
Adventure and joy dance, from morn until night.

The Lure of Evergreen Inspirations

In a forest where the trees all sway,
The squirrels gossip about the day.
They chat of pine cones and acorn dreams,
As sunlight dances and nature gleams.

The owls hoot jokes on the midnight trail,
While rabbits giggle, their laughter frail.
A deer joins in, with a leap and a spin,
Sharing puns about the grass so thin.

The trees wear hats of mossy delight,
While the frogs croak tunes through the starry night.
A bear does a jig, oh what a sight!
In the company of friends, everything's bright.

The whispers of leaves play the tune so grand,
A concert of nature, all joining hand.
With laughter as rhythm and leaves as sound,
In this merry place, joy is abound.

Dance of the Whispering Branches

The branches swirl in a breezy spree,
Dancing with laughter, so wild and free.
A parrot squawks a joke from above,
While chipmunks giggle, spreading the love.

Twisting and twirling like a merry ring,
The trees high-five, it's a playful fling.
With shadows that blend in a wacky parade,
Nature's own circus, where laughter won't fade.

The branches crack jokes, some hit, some miss,
And the sun plays along, it can't be amiss.
In this wacky world of quirky delight,
Every rustling leaf feels just so right.

So join in the dance, let your spirit soar,
As nature's own jesters perform evermore.
With smiles all around, it's a sight to see,
In this playful land, we all dance with glee.

Candles of Life in the Forest

In the twilight glow, the fireflies shine,
Like candles of laughter, all in a line.
They flicker and tease as they buzz around,
In this whimsical place where joy is found.

The mushrooms giggle as they grow in the night,
In hues of a rainbow, they're quite a sight!
With the breeze as their friend, they sway to the tune,
Under the watchful eye of the plump silver moon.

A raccoon in tuxedo sneaks by with a grin,
Offering acorns, "Come on, let's begin!"
With shadows and light, in this forest so bright,
It's a party of laughter, all bathed in twilight.

So raise your acorn cups, let's toast to the fun,
To the candles of laughter, our hearts they've won.
With every tiny flicker, we'll dance in delight,
In the jolly embrace of the magical night.

Interwoven Spirits of Nature

In this woodland dance, spirits intertwine,
The trees share secrets, oh how they shine!
With mischievous whispers, they plot and scheme,
Creating a ruckus, like a playful dream.

The butterflies flutter, with giggles galore,
While the hedgehogs roll, laughing on the floor.
Echoes of chuckles make the brook sway,
As crickets join in, with their chirping play.

The ferns wave hi from the forest's edge,
While the raccoons plot their nutty pledge.
"Let's throw a feast!" one cheeky squirrel squeaks,
With mischief in eyes and fun in their cheeks.

Together they frolic, so wild and bright,
In an orchestra of laughter beneath starlit night.
With spirits of nature, laughter runs free,
In this vibrant world, come and dance with me!

Seasons in a Leafy Embrace

In springtime, the trees hold a dance,
Their leaves waltz and prance in a glance.
But squirrels in suits add to the craze,
Debating whose nut is the best for the drays.

Summer sun brings a blanket so wide,
While raccoons argue, there's nowhere to hide.
With laughter and joy, they swim in the stream,
Planning a party, or so it would seem.

Then autumn rolls in with pumpkins so bright,
Leaves falling like confetti, quite a sight!
The chipmunks in costumes, a fashion show spree,
While owls can't stop laughing up in their tree.

Winter, oh winter, the chilly old chap,
Makes snowflakes giggle, each one with a cap.
As snowmen wobble and lose their cool,
The forest erupts in a snowball duel!

Age-Old Guardians of the Woods

Tall trees whisper secrets, they can't keep still,
While squirrels take bets on the acorns and thrill.
A wise old oak plays the part of the sage,
On topics like gossip and chasing young age.

The bearded elder speaks of the days gone by,
A tale of a tree that could touch the sky.
With laughter and joy, the branches entwine,
Agreeing that trees are just fine with some wine.

Beneath the green canopy, shadows abound,
With critters who've gathered, a merry-go-round.
They sing of their glory and giggle so loud,
Creating a ruckus, a jubilant crowd.

At night in the moonlight, they swap their tall tales,
While raccoons serve cocktails in acorn-filled pails.
Amongst ancient giants, the fun never stops,
Where laughter and wisdom make evergreen hops!

Echoes in the Ever-Bloom

In fields of bright colors, where chatter takes flight,
The flowers exchange puns till the fall of the night.
Bees buzz in sync to the rhythm of cheer,
While butterflies giggle, 'Do you pine for the deer?'

A daffodil claims it can dance on a breeze,
While roses just roll, enjoying the tease.
The daisies are flipping, their heads in the air,
Holding a contest for who'll win first hair!

As summer sweeps in, the petals are game,
They host a parade, with dancing their fame.
A peach tree named Pete is a master of pranks,
Baiting the bumblebees with treats in their banks.

In autumn's embrace, colors start to blend,
Pumpkins tell jokes, and the laughter won't end.
With nature chuckling, the echoes resound,
In this playful space where pure joy is found!

Tapestry of Everlasting Dreams

In a patch of blue sky, the clouds play charades,
While leaves spin around in their leafy cascades.
The giggles above chase the sun in delight,
As critters below hope they'll join in the flight.

A tapestry woven with laughter and cheer,
Every creature beneath knows the magic is near.
With wishes like dandelions, dust in the air,
The dreams of the woods tell a tale bold and rare.

From rabbits to moles, each one has a part,
Creating a canvas of rhythm and art.
With a wink and a nod, they meet at the brook,
Painting new dreams with each lively look.

As twilight approaches, the dance doesn't cease,
Stars twinkle above, spreading joy like a fleece.
In the heart of the woods, where the funliness thrives,
Tales spin in laughter, where nature arrives!

Chronicles of the Verdant Realm

Once a tree had a silly hat,
Worn by a squirrel who loved to chat.
He'd dance and twirl with glee in bloom,
While branches shook, causing quite the boom.

The flowers laughed at his fine attire,
While bees buzzed close, their wings on fire.
A jester barked from the leafy stage,
"Let's start a party! Let's engage!"

The trunk stood proud, but he turned red,
As acorns rained down, a nutty thread.
Together they laughed, each leaf in tow,
In the wind's embrace, their spirits would grow.

A concert began with a croaky frog,
Singing sweet tunes to entertain the bog.
With roots that wiggled, in playful dismay,
Life in the greenwood was a grand cabaret!

In the Embrace of Timeless Arbor

Once an oak claimed a mighty throne,
Wearing a crown made of twigs alone.
He swayed and swirled, said, "Look at me!
I'm the king of the forest, don't you see?"

With whispers of wind, the leaves took flight,
Said, "Your majesty, that's quite a sight!"
But a foghorn toad croaked from the mound,
"Your bark's much worse than your leaves, I've found!"

The saplings giggled, pranced in a line,
"Let's throw a fiesta; it'll be divine!"
With berries as snacks, and sap for the cheer,
The tallest of trees dodged a twig-filled spear!

They danced till the dusk, twirling around,
Each time they stepped, they'd trip on the ground.
From the roots to the crowns, laughter did swell,
In the world of the trees, all was quite well!

Beneath the Feathered Crown

Under the branches, a worm made a mat,
While birds perched above, gossiping like that.
"Did you see that fern? It thinks it's so grand,
But it tips over each time we take a stand!"

A butterfly joined, flapping with flair,
"Let's dance in the petals, and not a care!"
They twirled and they spun, in a riotous flight,
While the grass giggled softly, through day and night.

The sun sneezed down rays, a laugh in the air,
As critters all gathered for a daring dare.
"Who can hop highest?" a squirrel declared,
While the chimes of the leaves in applause prepared.

A raccoon popped in with a cheeky grin,
"I'll bet I can do it, but I'll need some gin!"
Amidst all the ruckus, the woodland thrived,
In a feathered fiesta, where joy was alive!

Tales of a Leafy Legacy

In a grove where the tall ferns rise,
A shy little sprout tried to disguise.
With a hat made of moss, he crept about,
"Just passing through," he squeaked, "no doubt!"

The daisies giggled, their petals aflutter,
"Don't cover your face; don't you feel nutter?"
But he wiggled and wobbled, right in the prance,
Hoping to join in the forest's dance.

A wise old willow with tales to tell,
Said, "Join us, young one; you'll fit in well!"
So he tossed off his mask and stepped right in,
With laughter erupting, they all did spin.

At twilight they feasted on acorns and pie,
As the moon grinned down with a twinkling eye.
So the leafy brigade, in their own leafy way,
Made memories that glittered at the close of day!

Secrets Beneath the Undergrowth

In the shadows of the green, so sly,
A squirrel plots his nutty heist nearby.
With acorns hidden in his secret lair,
He giggles softly, unaware of the bear.

Underneath the ferns and mossy beds,
Tiny creatures spin tales inside their heads.
A snail goes racing, slow as can be,
Bragging about his speed, quite comically.

The toad croaks loudly, the wise old sage,
Claims he's the star of the woodland stage.
But when a fly buzzes, he jumps in fright,
A clumsy dance beneath the moonlight.

Amongst the roots and twigs, they conspire,
Whispering secrets around the bonfire.
In this leafy world, a carnival shows,
Where laughter grows as the wildness flows.

Epiphany Under the Boughs

Beneath the branches, where shadows dive,
A raccoon wonders how to drive!
With paws at the wheel of a toy car,
He dreams of races, not going too far.

An owl with glasses, perched high with grace,
Reads the latest news in a woodland place.
He cackles and hoots, spills tea on the floor,
"Who needs a scoop? There's gossip galore!"

The fox plays poker with the crows in hats,
Dealing cards with nibble marks from his chats.
He bluffs and he grins, but oh what a fuss,
When the clever crows hold aces left to discuss!

An epiphany strikes, to laugh is the key,
In the wild's wacky life, carefree as a bee.
With every chuckle, the trees seem to sway,
Inviting us all to join in the play.

The Glistening Gaze of Nature

A butterfly twirls, a ballerina on air,
With sparkles and glimmers, her wings unaware.
She flits past the flowers, dressed up in style,
While ants march on, with not even a smile.

A chipmunk shows off, with peanuts in tow,
Strutting and fretting, that ego on show.
His friends roll their eyes, they know he's a tease,
For the biggest stash was up in a tree!

The river chuckles, with a bubbly glee,
Rippling over stones just as smooth as can be.
A fish jumps up high, thinking it's a clown,
Splashes down hard, then wears a frown.

Every rustle and whisper sings a bright song,
Nature's a jester, where laughter belongs.
In the glistening gaze, as life twirls around,
Joyful mischief is in every sound.

Essence of Life in Every Leaf

In every leaf hangs a secret delight,
A ladybug dances, full of pure light.
With polka dots proudly displayed on her back,
She twirls on a branch, no fear of attack.

A worm thinks he's wise as he wiggles his way,
Saying, "Life's just grand in the soil each day!"
But the earth shivers giggling at each little tease,
As the worm carries dreams far beneath the trees.

A bumblebee buzzes, no worries in tow,
With a feathered cap, puts on quite a show.
He dips down to sip from a flower and smear,
Dripping nectar all over—a sticky career!

In the arms of the trees, life's quirks intertwine,
Where laughter brings warmth and sunshine divine.
Essence spills over, like syrup on leaves,
Crafting a tapestry that joyfully weaves.

Requiem for the Evergreen Dream

In forests deep, the trees stand tall,
Forgotten dreams, they have a ball.
Swaying branches in the breeze,
They laugh at life, doing as they please.

Squirrels chatter, planning a feast,
While birds in their nests party, at least.
A deer in the shade writes a haiku,
About a leaf that got stuck in its shoe.

Mossy ground, a carpet so plush,
Rabbits with style, in a fashionable hush.
With dance moves that boggle the mind,
They break all the rules, and humanity's blind.

So raise a glass to the trees so green,
Who party like it's the best Halloween.
A requiem not for resting, oh no!
But for trees that love the show!

Dance of the Timeless Green

In a glade where the ferns take a twirl,
A critter jumps with a dizzying whirl.
The oak starts to sway, joining the fun,
While pine cones bounce, oh what a run!

The grasshoppers step with such flair,
While crickets play tunes without a care.
A raccoon moonwalks, a sight to see,
As trees root down for their jubilee.

Laughter ricochets off every leaf,
As wise old trunks share stories of grief.
But tonight's a laugh, no time for gloom,
They're shaking their branches, clearing the room.

So dance on, dear saplings, young and spry,
Under the moonlit, star-studded sky.
In this timeless grove, joy's the decree,
Join the dance, it's evergreen glee!

Whispers of Timeless Green

In the forest where secrets creep,
The trees share jokes while squirrels sleep.
"Why did the twig break?" one says with a grin,
"Because it couldn't handle the pressure within!"

Leaves rustle softly, a giggle in flight,
Pine needles snicker at stars shining bright.
"Moss grows faster, but we dance instead,
It's healthier here than eating plain bread!"

A woodpecker taps out a rhythmic beat,
As mushrooms join in for a funky treat.
"Why did the acorn apply for a job?
To prove he could be more than a mob!"

So be it, the whispers, the jokes, the cheer,
In the wonder of green, we hold so dear.
Nature's comedians, with humor so light,
In every whisper, there's laughter in sight!

Roots of Resilience

Deep in the earth, they dig and weave,
Roots of the trees, what do they believe?
"I've seen some things that would make you cringe,
Like last year's woodpecker trying to binge!"

A gnarled old oak, with branches so broad,
Claims resilience tips from his great-grandma nod.
"Never fret when winds come and go,
Just hold your ground, and put on a show!"

"Oh look, another storm's on the way,"
Said the willowy birch, in its fanciful sway.
"Just sway with the rhythm, don't fight the tide,
For a tree that can dance has nothing to hide!"

So here's to the roots, with humor and grace,
Growing stronger together, each steadfast embrace.
Through laughter and trials, they twist and twine,
In the heart of the forest, where spirits align!

Embrace of the Verdant Heart

In a forest of jokes, the trees wear a grin,
Whispering secrets where laughter begins.
Squirrels crack puns, with acorns in tow,
They dance with the branches, putting on a show.

With leaves like confetti, they cheerfully sway,
Moss-covered rocks join the frolicsome play.
Berries roll laughter down roots of the ground,
While breezes hum tunes, a very funny sound.

The owls hoot in rhythm, a wise guy refrain,
Telling tall tales of the oldest rain.
Each trunk holds a story, not one dull or dry,
As critters don costumes, oh me, oh my!

So come share a giggle in this leafy delight,
Where every green corner's a comic's invite.
With a wink from the ferns and a laugh from the pine,
This woodland of humor forever will shine.

The Pulse of the Evergreen Realm

In a kingdom of evergreens, laughter unfolds,
With pinecones as jesters, the humor it molds.
The boughs are the banners of giggles and glee,
While shadows throw parties on the roots of a tree.

Gentle chatter between the bushes does bloom,
Telling tall tales of a squirrel's costume.
Barking at bears who can't find their lost socks,
As chipmunks make dance moves that surprise and shock.

With every rustle, a new punchline drops,
Mossy-faced rocks settle down for some pops.
Each trunk is a witness to whimsical ways,
As laughter echoes through the green leafy maze.

So gallop through groves where the sun's rays collide,
And share in the chuckles that nature provides.
Amongst the tall giants, carry a tune,
For humor and nature are forever in tune.

Echoes of Life in the Shaded Hollow

In the shaded hollow where giggles do trace,
The shadows are busy in a merry race.
Chipmunks play tag with the drifting old leaves,
While sunbeams set up their fun little thieves.

The chatter of branches tickles the air,
As squirrels wear shades and laugh without care.
A frog jumps and croaks in a karaoke blare,
While crickets all join in, a chirpy affair.

Gather round laughter, let worries all cease,
For this grove of green is a riotous feast.
Where roots are the anchors of each funny tale,
And trees put on shows that could never fail.

So waltz with the woodpeckers, tap-dance with glee,
In the echoes of life, come be silly and free.
Under soft canopies, let your heart float,
For here in the hollow, the fun's always wrote.

Vows of the Evergreen Keeper

With vows to uphold, green guardian stands,
With a giggle and wink, and jokes on his hands.
His roots tie the world in a fun-loving way,
Spreading laughter like leaves on a bright sunny day.

Branches that chuckle at the weather's whims,
Find joy in the rain as each raindrop swims.
Bark wrapped in humor, knots twist and twirl,
Wildlife dances to the laughter they hurl.

He tells tales of mischief the critters all spread,
Like beavers in tuxedos or owls in their bed.
Every twinkle of sunlight brings nonsense galore,
As seeds of hilarity burst through every door.

So trust in the keeper, embrace all the fun,
Where greenery's laughter will never be done.
With winks from the pines and chuckles from thrush,
In this evergreen realm, life's a merry rush.